COFFEE TEA OR KOOL-AID

WHICH PARTY POLITICS ARE YOU SWALLOWING?

ERIN McHUGH

D1497104

Editor: David Cashion
Cover designer: Alissa Faden
Interior designer: Jessi Rymill
Production manager: Ankur Ghosh

ISBN 978-0-8109-9760-8

Library of Congress Cataloging-in-Publication Data available upon request.

Copyright © 2010 Erin McHugh

Published in 2010 by Abrams Image, an imprint of ABRAMS.

Printed and bound in U.S.A.

10 9 8 7 6 5 4 3 2 1

Abrams Image books are available at special discounts when purchased in
quantity for premiums and promotions as well as fundraising or educational use.
Special editions can also be created to specification. For details, contact
specialmarkets@abramsbooks.com, or the address below.

THE ART OF BOOKS SINCE 1949

115 West 18th Street
New York, NY 10011
www.abramsbooks.com

To everyone who's ever lobbied for something they wanted,
and to the rest of you who lie and say you never have.

CONTENTS

INTRODUCTION

In 2009, disgruntled Americans started a new grass-roots movement called the Tea Party, which quickly garnered a reputation for right-wing hijinks. Named after the Boston Tea Party of 1773, when colonists rose up against taxation without representation, the new Tea Party originally lashed out at President Obama, and specifically his economic stimulus package.

Protests, marches, even a convention sprung up, until suddenly it seemed the word "Teabagger" had been part of our vernacular forever. Then, on January 26, 2010, one lone Facebooker named Annabel Park, angered at the media's portrayal of right-wing Republicans as the only citizens who cared about government accountability and other issues that affect all of us, said Enough Already: "You don't have to be a Republican to be a patriot." And just like that, the Coffee Party was born. Since then, the Coffee Party Movement has toted up well over 200,000 Facebook followers, and reports are that each of its status updates gets around a million hits. Park & Friends' desire for civil discourse and community activism to begin to solve the problems this country faces has taken hold. It may be only a toehold, or we may find it's a very strong grip.

So…what'll it be, folks? It certainly is not voting as usual this year. People are picketing in knickers and tricorn hats; others are suggesting that you use your "inside voice" when talking politics. You'll discover invaluable information in these pages, a who's who of the movers and shakers behind the electoral scenes, from Sarah Palin to—believe it or not—Captain America. You'll also find signs and slogans, imagined scenarios from the front, even scientific (well, maybe quasi-scientific) observations in Venn diagram form. Craziness has consumed America's political imagination, and I invite you to join the fray.

This is the little book that spells it all out, and will help you laugh all the way to the polls. If you're casting a ballot this year, hang out here awhile first.

ERIN McHUGH
NEW YORK CITY

"IF WE COULD HAVE GOTTEN PEOPLE TO LISTEN **THEN,** WE WOULDN'T HAVE **DUG** THE HOLE AS DEEP AS IT IS **NOW.** IT'S **DONE** NOW **AND WE'VE GOT TO FIX IT.** THE SOONER WE START, THE BETTER OFF WE'LL BE. BUT **WE'VE GOTTA BE CAREFUL.**"

— ROSS PEROT

PARTY HISTORIES:

OR

HOW THINGS BEGAN TO BREW

KING GEORGE III

+

TAXATION

-

REPRESENTATION

=

BOSTON HARBOR

+

342 CHESTS OF TEA

1773

THE BOSTON TEA PARTY

"TAXATION WITHOUT REPRESENTATION!"

T his was the war cry of the colonists a full century and a half after the Pilgrims landed in Plymouth—but it took one particularly snarky group (same as it ever was) to put the whining to the test. The British American colonies were still under the thumb of King George III, and though the Townshend Acts—which taxed most items coming to the colonies—had been repealed, the pesky tax on tea still remained. (Wouldn't you know it? *So* British!) In other colonial ports, tea deliveries were being refused and promptly sent back across the pond. But the Bostonians would have none of it. When three ships came sailing in, full of the stuff, local patriot and Boston's Sons of Liberty leader Samuel Adams* riled up the locals, and soon enough they had a plan: do away with the cargo altogether.

So on December 16, 1773, angry men–some say thirty, many say a hundred more than that–stormed the ships and hoisted all 342 chests of tea over the side into Boston Harbor. Many of them had cleverly dressed as Indians, hoping to lay the blame on the purported Bad Guys. Oh, this felt good. This felt like a revolution brewing. And lo, very soon, it was. The Boston Tea Party and the resulting uproar, which included the King's closing of the port of Boston, helped plant the seeds of the American Revolution.

*** Yes, the real-life Samuel Adams was indeed a brewer, but there is no historical proof that this is why he masterminded getting rid of a competing beverage.**

BOSTON HARBOR

DECEMBER 16, 1773

1 BOX = 10 CHESTS of TEA

THE TEA PARTY MOVEMENT

"TAXED ENOUGH ALREADY"

Hard on the heels of the first days of Barack Obama's presidency in 2009, bands of angry, sore-loser conservatives began to take the new president's stimulus plan–designed to alleviate the greatest economic downturn since the Great Depression–personally. Nor were they pleased with the mortgage and bank bailouts in the late days of the Bush administration.

Though opinions differ on where the first folks congregated under the Tea Party name, certainly this new movement was boiling by mid-February.

Ever since 1773, the original Boston Tea Party has been cited as an early successful American direct action, the Holy Grail of libertarians and anti-tax conservatives. So when Fox Business Network's Dave Ramsey held up some tea bags on the air and proclaimed "It's time for a tea party," well, that was all some people needed to hear. Angry citizens, proclaiming that TEA stood for "Taxed Enough Already," took to sending actual tea bags to their legislators, to the White House, to whomever they thought might listen. (This brought about the unfortunate and snickersome nickname, Teabaggers, which we will address anon.)

The main divergence here, as the New Tea Party pays verbal homage to the Real Tea Party, is that taking up the "Taxation Without Representation" cry is

> 66 Stop calling the Tea Party phenomenon a movement. To be a real political movement you have to, well, move, towards some specific legislative goal. The suffrage movement, for example, gave voting rights for women. The civil rights movement outlawed discrimination against blacks. And the gay rights movement brought us the Winter Olympics. But the Tea Baggers – they're not a movement. They're a cult. 99
>
> —BILL MAHER, PUNDIT

misrepresentation in itself. Nowadays we have congresspeople and senators—lots of them, too!—in every district of these United States. Back in the Samuel Adams days, what the angry mob demanded made sense: Here we are, working for The Man (King George), with no say about how our lives are governed. That's different than just not liking who gets elected. This is not the same

YOUR POLITICAL GLOSSARY
PORKULUS

Let's give this cartoonish word a little bit of class for a moment.

PORKULUS is what's called a *portmanteau*, which is a word that is a blend of two others. Brunch (breakfast + lunch) is a portmanteau, as are other fancy words like Oxbridge (Oxford + Cambridge) and croissandwich (croissant + sandwich).

PORKULUS has no such highbrow history. This new word comes from the marriage of pork + stimulus. In this instance, pork is "a legislative appropriation designed to ingratiate legislators with their constituents," as one definition goes. Stimulus refers, of course, to President Obama's stimulus package (technically the American Recovery and Reinvestment Act of 2009). It is used mostly with disdain, as in, "I can't believe that Communist Obama is giving away my hard-earned money to bums with that porkulus package of his."

The word is attributed to Rush Limbaugh, who in his January 28, 2009 show, referred to Obama's new "porkulus package." It was the 2009 Stimulus Act that prompted the formation of the Tea Party.

as no self-governance. Perhaps a more accurate slogan for the Tea-baggers is "I Hate Not Getting My Way."

What else do they want? Well, they'd like to have all Republican government legislators—or independents, as long as they're conservative—from 1600 Pennsylvania Avenue on down. Aside from their wish for coast-to-coast domination, they're upset about Big Government, concerned with fiscal responsibility, and want fewer taxes, taxes, taxes. That taxes help pay for the Social Security and Medicare they enjoy simply does not seem to compute.

Nevertheless, the Tea Party movement has grown like Topsy, and in a paean to the Original Tea Party, its members often dress in colorful historical garb

> 66 We know who we are against. We don't quite know who we are for yet. 99
>
> —JUSTIN HOLLAND, ORGANIZER FOR THE NORTH ALABAMA PATRIOT TEA PARTY

at their meetings and hoedowns, creating a sea of ranting Uncle Sams and Paul Reveres. And they have real, *living* celebrities on hand, too. Like former Speaker of the House Newt Gingrich, Sean Hannity of Fox News, and the foxy ex-governor of the frozen state of Alaska, Sarah Palin.

And of course, they have Sam Adams—the beer, not the Son of Liberty.

BOSTON TEA PARTY	TEA PARTY MOVEMENT

FIGURE 1

RIGHTEOUS INDIGNATION

$+$

NETROOTS ACTIVISM

$+$

CIVIL DISCOURSE

STAR POWER & BIG MONEY

$=$

THE COFFEE PARTY

THE COFFEE PARTY

"WAKE UP AND STAND UP"

One cold winter night–January 26, 2010, to be exact–an angry documentary filmmaker named Annabel Park logged on to Facebook, like countless other people across the USA. But Park typed in a message that became, as Rachel Maddow called it on her show, "the Facebook status update heard round the world."

Annabel Park let's start a coffee party . . . smoothie party. red bull party. anything but tea. geez. ooh how about cappuccino party? that would really piss 'em off bec it sounds elitist . . . let's get together and drink cappuccino and have real political dialogue with substance and compassion.
January 26 at 9:36 p.m.

"Friends of mine online bonded immediately," Park recalls. "Within about half an hour of that rant I created this fan page, 'Join the Coffee Party Movement.'" The page got over 600,000 clicks the first week. And just like that, the Coffee Party was born.

Park was sick and tired of seeing the media (read: Fox News) portray right-wing Americans as the only citizens who could be considered patriots. In fact, a lot of the issues the Tea Party addresses are on the Coffee Party agenda as well—government accountability, money in politics, Wall Street reform, and the like.

But the Coffee Party folks are not haters. Racism, homophobia, and "baby killers" are not spoken here, as they so often are by Tea Party extremists. In fact, civil discourse is the watchword of the java crowd. And there couldn't be any better example of how much that civility is needed than the Teabagging misbehavior witnessed outside the Capitol during the health care reform debates in March 2010. Spitting, name-calling, and threats are not the Coffee Party's cup of tea. Park and the Coffee Party want to heal America's relationship with its own government, and insist that Coffee Party members and meetings rely on open dialogue, discussion, and cooperation. The Coffee Party is built to be the epitome of grassroots activism.

Well, not so fast. Not everybody's convinced of that last statement. Park's a brainiac, no doubt about it: She even went to Oxford as a Marshall Scholar. But within weeks of the Coffee Party's formation, Teabaggers and other naysayers were insisting that she is not the altruist she purports to be. She volunteered for the Obama presidential campaign—innocent enough in some peoples' eyes, high treason to others. Teabaggers are eager to point out that Park worked at the *New York Times* (over a decade ago, and not in the news department) and claim she is under the thumb of Virginia senator Jim Webb and billionaire George Soros (the Coffee Party Facebook page explains it all away as sharing and donation of free Internet services). Lastly, she's something lots of Teabaggers are very suspicious of: foreign. Park was born in Korea and moved here with her family as a child. (No birth certificate question here.)

The Coffee Party has all the hallmarks of an aw-shucks, earnest college sit-in, complete with wonky spokesperson and lots of righteous indignation. Plenty of talk, no money, snail-paced plans for action. No tour bus, no glamourpussy starlet frontchick with upswept hairdo.

Is this brew strong enough to become more than a kaffeeklatsch?

66 We need to roll up our sleeves and work together. Nothing will change in Washington or on Wall St. if we continue to focus on fighting each other. We are like a husband and wife fighting each other to the bitter end while the basement is flooding and thieves are plundering the house. Who cares who wins the fight if there is nothing left in the house and we are drowning. 99

—COFFEE PARTY USA FACEBOOK PAGE

2009

KOOL-AID

"DON'T BE AFRAID TO DIE"

Fruit Smack probably didn't have much of a future as a brand name. Maybe on a little glassine package of heroin, but not for a tot's sippy cup. But that's what Edwin and Kitty Perkins called the drink they were cooking up in his mama's kitchen back in Nebraska while the rest of the country was whooping it up during the Roaring Twenties. Realizing it was too expensive to ship as a liquid, Perkins dreamed up a way to extract just the powder and–*voilà!*–Kool-Aid was born. Since then, Kool-Aid has been the staple of millions of birthday parties, though nary a political one.

Now negative publicity–even the unfounded variety–can bring down a sweet, innocent reputation, both in a snacky-treat or in politics. Long a staple of old-fashioned summer fun, Kool-Aid began to run with a wild crowd. First, in the 1960s, a new concoction of Kool-Aid became the cocktail of choice for the likes of Ken Kesey and his Merry Pranksters, the Grateful Dead, and writer Tom Wolfe. Electric Kool-Aid, it was called—a combo of Kool-Aid (any flavor) laced with LSD. The story of these legendary experiments is recounted in Wolfe's *The Electric Kool-Aid Acid Test,* called "simply the best book on hippies" by the *New York Times.* Hippies. Just the audience Kool-Aid was looking for!

Kool-Aid's now-tarnished reputation took an even more disastrous hit a decade later, when a delegation of American politicians and concerned family members traveled to Jonestown, Guyana, to check on worrisome reports of cult leader Jim Jones and his Peoples Temple. When Jones realized his visitors were leaving Guyana armed with tales of forced imprisonment and a likely call for action by the United States government, he urged his followers to commit "revolutionary suicide" by drinking preprepared doses of Kool-Aid laced with cyanide. Nine hundred and fourteen people died that day at the Peoples Temple Agricultural Project by the virtual hand of Jim Jones. Today, "drinking the Kool-Aid," meaning to blindly accept another's opinion or philosophy as truth, has become part of the American vernacular. Some would say this is the way of all politics.

But the real killer is this: Upon further inspection, it so happens the delivery system for the poison was not Kool-Aid at all, but a copycat product called Flavor Aid. Oh, the unwarranted stigma! The shame brought upon that jolly, thirst-quenching pitcher with the ever-ready smile! Well played, Flavor Aid. And that's how you win elections.

THE STORY OF DWAYNE W.

Hi . . . my name is Dwayne, and I'm a Teabagger.

"Hi, Dwayne!!!!"

I can't even really remember how I started getting into Teabagging. I mean, I've been a Republican all my life. Hell, I come from four generations of Republicans. But it was only social—you know, country-club Republicans. I only talked about politics when I drank. It was just for fun . . . it kept things exciting.

"Then what happened, Dwayne?"

Well, I guess just being a Republican wasn't enough. It got dull. And then along came Sarah Palin.

She was beautiful. She was exotic—I mean, she lived in *Alaska*! She loved guns, and she wasn't afraid to talk about them. My wife . . . well, I love my wife, don't get me wrong—but she won't even let our little boy have a squirt gun.

Suddenly, being a Republican seemed sort of . . . sexy. But then Sarah got involved with this Tea Party, and I couldn't stop myself: I went along. There was a bus tour—it was called the Tea Party Express—and I left my family and signed up as a roadie. All us volunteers were the same. Well, actually, I left my job as a CPA, but lots of the other roadies and hangers-on were out of work and mad as hell.

We hated Obamacare. We were paying taxes, and people with nothing were getting health care! That didn't seem right. Of course, I was too drunk on Sarah Palin to realize that my taxes were also paying for my own Social Security and Medicare and, soon enough, my unemployment. All I saw was the fun of picketing, name-calling, and phone threats.

It was exciting in a way I never knew possible.

"What finally happened, Dwayne? What brought you to Teabaggers Anonymous?"

I hit rock bottom. I found myself in Washington, D.C., in front of the Capitol, the bastion of all we hold dear, spitting at a congressman, screaming things at him that I would ground my kids for until they were fifty.

Right then and there, I took off my Uncle Sam hat, burned my Glenn Beck books, and came straight to T.A.

I'm looking for a kinder, gentler America. Where there's civil discourse, and people really sit down and talk to each other. I've heard about this Coffee Party . . .

"Don't do it, Dwayne! It's just substituting one addiction for another!"

No, no, I'm sure I can handle it. I'll just go to a Coffee Party meeting and see what they have to say. I'll just have a tiny taste . . .

PARTY
MISSION
STATEMENTS

MISSION STATEMENT: COFFEE PARTY

"**T**he Coffee Party Movement gives voice to Americans who want to see cooperation in government. We recognize that the federal government is not the enemy of the people, but the expression of our collective will, and that we must participate in the democratic process in order to address the challenges we face as Americans. As voters and grassroots volunteers, we will support leaders who work toward positive solutions, and hold accountable those who obstruct them."

And the Coffee Party Facebook page does ask members—guess it's on the honor system—to take the Coffee Party Pledge:

"As a member or supporter of the Coffee Party, I pledge to conduct myself in a way that is civil, honest, and respectful toward people with whom I disagree. I value people from different cultures, I value people with different ideas, and I value and cherish the democratic process."

YOUR POLITICAL GLOSSARY
ASTROTURFING

Both the Coffee and Tea parties have pointed fingers at each other on the question of ASTROTURFING. Funny word. What does it mean? Surely not the inside of a sports stadium! But it is a play on words, the direct opposite of grassroots. Whereas grassroots work is organizing done by a community of concerned citizens, usually on a volunteer basis, astroturfing is political action designed to *look* as if its source is "the people." Generally astroturfing campaigns are designed and run by corporations, lobbyists, or other political interest groups. The right has accused the Coffee Party of being under the thumb of billionaire George Soros, though investigations seem to bear out that they merely use a firm funded by Soros called Democracy in Action, a nonprofit company that offers free website services to progressive 501(c)(3) groups. The left declares astroturfing to be at the heart of the entire Tea Party movement.

The word is thought to have been first uttered by Senator Lloyd Bentsen (D-TX) back in 1985, when a suspicious number of letters concerning a single issue reached his office. He opined, "A fellow from Texas can tell the difference between grass roots and Astroturf. This is generated mail."

MISSION STATEMENT: TEA PARTY MOVEMENT

★ ★ ★ ★ ★ ★ ★  ★ ★ ★ ★ ★ ★

The Tea Party Patriots (http://www.teapartypa-triots.org/), one of the largest Tea Party groups, have taken a giant organizational step in drawing up their Contract from America, presented on Tax Day, April 15, 2010, at a rally at the Washington Monument. Though nary a one of us will be fooled by the suspiciously familiar ring of its name, Tea Party Patriots are viewing this to-do list as all new, and warn that it should not be confused with the 1994 Gingrichian manifesto, Contract with America. The percentages denote the number of voters who went online and cast a virtual ballot as to what they "encourage congressional candidates to follow." The website touts that 454,331 votes were cast.

82.03% **IDENTIFY CONSTITUTIONALITY OF EVERY NEW LAW:** Require each bill to identify the specific provision of the Constitution that gives Congress the power to do what the bill does.

72.20% **REJECT EMISSIONS TRADING:** Stop the "cap and trade" administrative approach used to control pollution by providing economic incentives for achieving reductions in the emissions of pollutants.

69.69% **DEMAND A BALANCED FEDERAL BUDGET:** Begin the Constitutional amendment process to require a balanced budget with a two-thirds majority needed for any tax modification.

64.90% **ENACT FUNDAMENTAL TAX REFORM:** Adopt a single-rate tax system; eliminate the internal revenue code and replace it with one that is no longer than 4,543 words.

63.37% **AUDIT FEDERAL GOVERNMENT AGENCIES FOR CONSTITUTIONALITY:** Create a blue-ribbon taskforce that engages in a complete audit of federal agencies and programs, assessing their constitutionality, and identifying duplication, waste, ineffectiveness, and agencies and programs better left for the states or local authorities.

56.57% **LIMIT ANNUAL GROWTH IN FEDERAL SPENDING:** Impose a statutory cap limiting the annual growth in total federal spending to the sum of the inflation rate plus the percentage of population growth.

56.39%   **DE-FUND, REPEAL, AND REPLACE THE HEALTHCARE LEG-ISLATION PASSED ON MARCH 23, 2010:** De-fund, repeal and replace the Patient Protection and Affordable Care Act.

55.5%   **PASS AN "ALL-OF-THE-ABOVE" ENERGY POLICY:** Authorize the exploration of proven energy reserves to reduce American dependence on foreign energy sources and reduce regulatory barriers to all other forms of energy creation.

55.47%   **REDUCE EARMARKS:** Place a moratorium on all earmarks until the budget is balanced, and then require a two-thirds majority to pass any earmark.

53.38%   **REDUCE TAXES:** Permanently repeal all recent tax increases, including those to the income tax, capital gains, and estate taxes, currently scheduled to begin in 2011.

YOUR POLITICAL GLOSSARY
NETROOTS

NETROOTS is the newer, slicker, ever-changing grandbaby of grassroots: political organizing through different aspects of the Internet, whether it be social networking websites, blogs, or other new avenues to reach an increasingly more sophisticated audience.

MISSION
STATEMENT:
KOOL-AID

★ ★ ★ ★ ★ ★  ★ ★ ★ ★ ★ ★

O f course a soft drink rarely has a mission statement—at least not one parent company Kraft
Foods is likely to let the public in on—but where
there's a product, there's a slogan, and apparently time heals all wounds.

After many years of using:

"Moms depend on Kool-Aid like kids depend on Moms!"

Kraft decided to put the whole nasty Jonestown thing aside
and opt for a brighter outlook:

"Delivering more smiles per gallon."

Ouch.

IMMIGRATION!

CLIMATE CHANGE!

TAXES!

EVERYONE HAS ISSUES

Coffee Party founder Annabel Park's initial observation was right: America is chock-full of patriots of every stripe and color—not just the Fox News Right. And although there are bound to be as many opinions as there are people, some issues matter to everyone, from the liberal left to the radical right. It's how they view these issues that keep the Washington juices running.

> 66 We're not the opposite of the Tea Party. We're a different model of civic participation, but in the end we may want some of the same things. 99

—ANNABEL PARK, COFFEE PARTY FOUNDER

Patrik Jonsson from the *Christian Science Monitor* commented wisely on what seem to be sometimes vague differences between the Coffee and Tea folks:

❝ The Coffee Party USA may as well be the Communist Party USA. ❞

—NH TEA PARTY COALITION

"Even if the messages sound the same, the two movements differ in substantive ways. Tea Partyers tend to berate the federal government as a whole (or most of it). Coffee Partyers seem to be more in favor of government involvement—as in envisioning a greater role for government in the future of healthcare—but denounce the 'corporatocracy' that holds sway in Washington."

Here are some of the more vital issues both parties frequently address:

GOVERNMENT ACCOUNTABILITY

Often, this issue seems simply a matter of semantics. To generalize, the Coffee Party firmly believes that the government is not the enemy, but a tool of the people—the accountability they speak of generally refers to reporting back to constituents and inclusiveness in governmental decision-making. For the Tea Party, accountability means dollars and cents, as in, "Where did our hard-earned tax dollars go?"

IMMIGRATION REFORM

Most every citizen will agree that immigration reform needs to be addressed immediately, but rarely has anything put a face on people's feelings about this subject the way the signing of the immigration bill in Arizona did in the spring of 2010. This was an instance where the Tea and Coffee Parties stood almost exclusively on opposite sides of the fence. The Teabaggers backed Governor Jan Brewer's bill, which allows law enforcement officials to stop anyone they suspect is an illegal immigrant and demand identification. The more liberal Coffee Partyers are horrified, insisting that it is one big invitation for racial profiling.

FREE MARKETS

The buying and selling of products without intervention from the government—in short, capitalism—has been one of the basic tenets of these United States, and is not likely to soon disappear. Neither the left nor the right expect this to change (except, naturally, the more rabid Teabaggers, who are quite certain that the diabolical Barack Obama's evil plan will soon result in a Communist state). However, more conservative voters will say we have stepped over the line with the passage of health care reform and situations such as resuscitating the failing auto industry. Is the road to socialism really paved with good intentions?

TAXES

This one is as old as the two-party system. Liberals will likely always lean toward helping citizens in need, supporting government programs that benefit less fortunate people; and the mantra "Taxed Enough Already" is the T-E-A in Tea Party. 'Nuff said there.

CLIMATE CHANGE

Several recent polls have shown Republicans to be less interested in climate change and environmental issues in general—and yet, there are also those on the right who believe there *is* no climate change problem. And though there has been some recent concern among conservatives about capping carbon monoxide emissions, they are generally the "Drill, baby, drill" crowd as well. The Coffee Party, being composed primarily of lefties, is, of course, home to a greener crowd.

A DAY IN THE LIFE OF AN ACTIVIST

Maybe the Teabaggers and these Coffee folks aren't so different from each other, you may be thinking to yourself. They both put their pants on one leg at a time, right? But then what's the rest of their day like after they peck their beloved on the cheek and head out into the world? We decided to find out and xeroxed a page from an activist's book—or rather, a day each from both a Tea Party member and a Coffee Partyer. Changing the world makes for a busy day!

COFFEE PARTYER

09:00a	Bookstore: get *How to Win Friends and Influence People*
10:00a	BANK: Deposit donations (don't forget change in sock drawer)
11:00a	Etiquette lessons/Emily Post Institute
12:00p	Lunch: Suzanne from Paperworks— ask about bartering coffee for free paper?
3:00p	Call CELEBRITY IMPERSONATOR PLACE for prices: * Michelle Obama * Ted Kennedy * Madonna
6:00p	Adult Education seminar—"Loving the Hater: Survive Name-calling, Spitting, and Other Bad Behavior"
8:00p	Update Facebook page
9:00p	Edit footage for new doc: "How to Keep a Civil Tongue"

TEA PARTYER

Kinko's—pick up leaflets.
REFUSE TO PAY FOR first 3 ROUNDS WITH MISTAKES!!

Piggly Wiggly—tea bags!!!

Adult Education seminar—"Political Math:
How to Make Numbers and Polls Read Your Way"

H&R Block: recheck tax numbers—paying too much!!!

Bank—deposit unemployment and Social Security checks

Pick up new Tea Party Express tour bus at dealer's

Bible prayer group

Hatmaking class—tricorn this week!

**send speaker fee to Palin!

MEET
THE
BIGWIGS!

Say what you want about straight, rich, white men running the United States government, and then take a look at the two people who are credited with being the first to get the Tea Party and the Coffee Party percolating. The first thing you might notice? They're both young women. And, coincidentally, they both studied at Oxford. Already this looks like a change is gonna come. Herein, a look at some of the bigwigs.

WHO'S WHO OF **TEA PARTY** BIGWIGS

KELI CARENDER, THE BLOGGER

Nearly every write-up about KELI CARENDER notes: She has tattoos! A nose ring! Works for a nonprofit! Does *improv!* To the MSM (aka mainstream media), this seems to spell out L-I-B-E-R-A-L, but in fact Carender, who hails from Seattle, is actually credited with starting the Tea Party. Even "leaders of the Tea Party movement credit her with being the first," says the *New York Times.* Blogging as Liberty Belle and flipped out about President Obama's stimulus package, she got on the web, the horn, and the rooftops to arrange a protest in downtown Seattle on February 16, 2009. About 120 folks showed up, and the Tea Party was out of the gate.

MARK WILLIAMS, THE INSTIGATOR

MARK WILLIAMS is a longtime conservative radio host who has put his extremely controversial style and pronouncements to work as chairman of the Tea Party Express. Though he insists that the Tea Party movement is a "battle for the soul of America," Williams has spoken so outrageously in the past that even some of the more extreme Teabaggers shy away. He evidently has a thing for authority, calling Jimmy Carter "a slithering worm of a man" who "longs for an oven of fresh-baked Jews," due to his work with Arabic leaders. Williams has called George W. Bush a "Klansman in black face," and President Obama an "Indonesian Muslim turned welfare thug" and "racist-in-chief." In his attempts to win friends and influence people, he apparently could not find a reputable publisher, and has self-published his own story: *Mark Williams: Taking Back America One Tea Party at a Time.*

DICK ARMEY, THE LOBBYIST

He is a man with a past—and what a past. Though now registered as a lobbyist in Washington, DICK ARMEY came out of North Dakota, a state known as the home of some great American women—Sacagawea, Peggy Lee, Angie Dickinson—but not many men of renown. Armey challenged all that when he came to Capitol Hill as a congressman in 1985, though he was by then a Texan. Reelected eight times, his power grew exponentially, as did his problems with women charging him with sexual harassment (somehow, sex and Washington never seem to make strange bedfellows). Armey's most important contribution to end-of-century politics, however, was his work with Newt Gingrich in constructing the famous Contract with America and bringing the Republicans back into power on Capitol Hill in 1994. When Gingrich became

> 66 No man can ever lose his daddy's spurs. 99
>
> —DICK ARMEY

Speaker of the House, Armey was suddenly House majority leader. Not bad for nine years work.

First hint of Teabagging leanings? Perhaps when he "mistakenly" called Congressman Barney Frank "Barney Fag." Today, Armey is chairman of one of the Tea Party's strongest allies, FreedomWorks, a Washington nonprofit whose website states its mission is to drive "policy change by training and mobilizing grassroots Americans to engage their fellow citizens and encourage their political representatives to act in defense of individual freedom and economic opportunity." FreedomWorks is often accused of astroturfing, and always denies it.

SARAH PALIN, THE BABE

SARAH PALIN is the epitome of someone who needs no introduction. A mayor, a governor—and still an unknown—she blew onto the political stage and very nearly got laughed off while still in the running for vice president. The irony is quintessentially American: She is impersonated on national TV, and then becomes a serious news commentator. She speaks of hunting and killing animals, then gets a show on the Discovery Channel. There have been jokes about bringing Paris Hilton on board for the 2012 Bimbo Ticket. Palin has been called many, many things, but "Ross Perot 2.0" may be the most complimentary.

Many say Sarah Palin is driving the Tea Party Express—the movement, not the bus. Whether she and other Republican and Tea Party patriots actually consider the Tea Party to be a viable third party remains to be seen. The feeling from much of the Republican Party is that it would be nothing but divisive.

COFFEE, TEA, or KOOL-AID 47

MICHELE BACHMANN, THE OTHER BABE

There's a new Fox, er, fox in town, Ms. Palin—and her name is MICHELE
BACHMANN. Don't be surprised if Farrah Fawcett–like posters of this Min-
nesota congresswoman start appearing on the bedroom walls of middle-
aged Republican men all over America. After Tax Day Tea Party protests,
she said on the Fox Business Network that "if you go to one of the tea party
rallies, they're actually the happiest people you would ever want to meet.
It's almost like going to a state fair, to a family reunion." Bachmann has
also stated that the Tea Party and the
Republican Party are "really merg-
ing into one single, solitary unit . . .
They have unified." Stay tuned. She
evidently knows something the rest
of us don't.

> 66 I'd say it's time for these little piggies to
> go home. 99
>
> —MICHELE BACHMANN (ON CONGRES-
> SIONAL DEMOCRATS)

❧ ❧ ❧ THE MEDIA ❧ ❧ ❧

GLENN BECK ❧

Whether dressed as a stormtrooper on the cover of his book, *Arguing with
Idiots,* or talking about his role as a top conservative radio and TV host ("I
could give a flying crap about the political process"), GLENN BECK succeeds
like mad at riling folks up. Though he is a fave among Tea Partyers in their
quest for a fearless leader, Beck seems more interested in his 9-12 Project,
whose purpose, he says, is "to bring us all back to the place we were on
Sept. 12, 2001." Beck spells out nine Principles and twelve Values, which he

says are not party-affiliated, but anti–big government. Though the Values are fairly straightforward and appealing to nearly everyone—they include Hard Work, Honesty, Courage, and Hope—the Principles might find a smaller audience: "I believe in God and He is the Center of my Life."

ANN COULTER

ANN COULTER, author and syndicated columnist, says she "likes to stir up the pot," and she certainly has, on the printed page, on national TV, and now as a Tea Party spokeswoman, even appearing on the road with the Palin Posse. Coulter's own website has a list of "Reporters Who Are Allowed to Interview Ann Again." There are seven. Chances are good that the rest of the journalistic world has simply vamoosed. Chat with Ann Coulter, and you take your life in your hands.

SEAN HANNITY

SEAN HANNITY is a Fox man, and nearly deep-sixed the Fox News slogan of "Fair and Balanced" when he charged admission for a taping of his show, which was filming at a Tea Party rally, with proceeds to go to the Teabaggers. Big Boss Rupert Murdoch got wind of the plan. "I don't think we should be supporting the Tea Party, or any other party," said the conservative network king, leaving Hannity out to dry.

RUSH LIMBAUGH

In many quarters, RUSH LIMBAUGH's promise to leave the United States if health care reform passed was greeted with huzzahs. For others, who made his radio show the highest-rated in the country, it threatened the end of a cherished era. In either case, Obamacare is here, and Limbaugh's talk of a future in Costa Rica seems to have mysteriously subsided. This means Limbaugh is still the Voice of God to many, and he's all Tea Party, all the time.

BILL O'REILLY

Whereas Limbaugh has the biggest number of conservative ears, the eyes have it in the guise of BILL O'REILLY: Fox News Channel's *The O'Reilly Factor* is the most watched cable news show in the country. O'Reilly does seem to be one of the only media folks on the right who consistently advises the Tea Partyers to try to tone down the rhetoric of their more rambunctious compatriots. O'Reilly is a registered independent, like many who have turned to the Tea Party for answers and solace.

RICK SANTELLI

RICK SANTELLI, the financial trader–turned-newscaster, was reporting for CNBC in the Windy City on February 19, 2009. Having learned of President Obama's Homeowners Affordability and Stability Plan to help save Americans from foreclosures, he exclaimed that perhaps what was needed was a Chicago Tea Party. There have been suspicions that his outburst was staged, and that it was a little bit of Howard Beale redux. Movie buffs of a certain age will remember *Network* and the famous line of Beale's, a role that won Peter Finch a posthumous Oscar:

"I'm mad as hell, and I'm not going to take it anymore!"
This has become one of the Tea Party's real-life mantras.

🍵 VICTORIA JACKSON, THE COMEDIAN

VICTORIA JACKSON? Seriously? Someone you haven't even thought of in a dozen years—and yet you remember her so fondly!—is back in the limelight *here?* What happened to her funny bone? On Tax Day, she was seen in patriotic costume singing, "Everybody! There's a Communist living in the White House!" Perhaps it all became suddenly more clear when she stated, "But if you believe in Christ and that your main goal with your life is supposed to be to honor Him and do His will, then you don't have as much pressure as someone who bases all their happiness on whether they're a movie star." Hmmm. Or maybe not so clear.

YOUR POLITICAL GLOSSARY
BIRTHERS

"Show us the birth certificate!" is still the war cry of a group of American conspiracy theorists bent on disproving the citizenship of Barack Obama. Article Two of the Constitution rules that our president must be a natural born citizen of the United States, and Tea Party folks in particular have been insistent that the president was not born in Hawaii at all, but in Kenya or, perhaps, Indonesia. Copies of Obama's birth certificate don't deter them ("It's just a copy"), and their attempts at litigation (e.g., he's not eligible to be United States president because he had dual citizenship at birth) have been foiled over and over again.

🍵 🍵 🍵 🍵   WHO'S WHO OF **COFFEE PARTY** BIGWIGS   🍵 🍵 🍵 🍵

ANNABEL PARK, THE ACTIVIST   🍵

As far as "new media" is concerned, ANNABEL PARK seems quaintly old-fashioned (although let's remember she began the whole Coffee Party phenomenon on Facebook).

Park is a longtime political activist, and she has been at the heart of a grassroots movement once before. In 2007, she became the national co-ordinator for House Resolution 121 (which passed with her help that year), known as the Comfort Women Resolution, concerning the sexual enslavement of Korean and other women by the Japanese during World War II. She is a documentary filmmaker whose *9500 Liberty,* made with partner Eric Byler, has won several awards. Agree with her or not, Park leads an extremely earnest life, fraught with enormous questions of right and wrong.

ERIC BYLER, THE DOCUMENTARY FILMMAKER   🍵

ERIC BYLER, Park's partner in love and political action, has garnered both praise and awards for his filmmaking since his college senior thesis. His talents immediately came in handy when Park's Facebook rant turned into a movement almost overnight, and he has directed several videos promoting the Coffee Party. He codirected the award-winning *9500 Liberty* mentioned previously, a movie about how a change in just

 The swing voters—I like to refer to them as the idiot voters because they don't have set philosophical principles. You're either a liberal or you're a conservative if you have an IQ above a toaster. 99

—ANN COULTER

one law can tear a community apart. Ironically, it's all about small government—just what the folks in the Tea Party yearn for!—and yet it speaks to something the Teabaggers are mightily concerned with: immigration reform. This film, which takes place in Prince William County, Virginia, echoes nearly exactly the recent immigration bill in Arizona and the reaction of local citizens.

YOUR POLITICAL GLOSSARY
TEABAGGING

And now we approach a more sensitive issue: a term that has its roots in sexual foreplay, yet now enjoys a second life as a part of the Tea Party vernacular, partly due to its members' political actions, and partly out of pure malice on the left.

TEABAGGING originated as a name for the action of putting one's scrotum in the mouth of a sexual partner; moving it in and out repeatedly is reminiscent of dipping a tea bag in a cup of Earl Grey. But this activity is not always consensual—it has become a form of hazing.

So really, how could the left and the media resist when the Tea Party folks themselves started sending tea bags to politicians' offices to show their strength in numbers. This new group was asking for it, weren't they?

And yet: Despite the ridicule, in the sexual sense, it is the male whose genitals are being serviced who is considered the Teabagger. The alpha male, the one in charge. So beware, liberal left.

☕ / 🫖 /☕ / 🫖 SIPPING FROM BOTH CUPS ☕ / 🫖 / ☕/ 🫖

AL ALBORN, THE LOBBYIST

Most Tea Party members are Republicans, but there are many disaffected independents in their midst as well. And every once in a while a real anomaly pops up, like independent voter AL ALBORN, who has become a spokesman for the Coffee Party. Alborn has held executive positions at Fortune 500 companies—and has more than twenty years in the Army under his belt. As seen in a Coffee Party USA video, Alborn is a combination of all-American and Army central casting—tough-talking, steely-haired, two obedient dogs by his side. The film even opens showing the two-story log cabin where he lives, Stars and Stripes waving in the breeze out front. Inside, Alborn is in civilian clothes, all Army beige.

"I believe the only rules we need are don't hurt other people and don't take their stuff," Alborn says in an interview about his perhaps surprising involvement with the Coffee Party. "I'm watching the various movements—the Tea Party movement, the Coffee Party movement, and trying to figure out where I fit. On the surface the Tea Party says a lot of good things: free markets, smaller government, lower taxes—but that's yesterday's story."

The man who says his favorite Amendment is the Tenth ("The powers not delegated to the United States by the Constitution nor prohibited to it by the states are reserved to the states respectively, or to the people") is suddenly reflective: "I'm starting to see government's role as a regulatory role. We need to figure out how to come together and advance the process of government. And that's what's broke right now."

Then along came Annabel Park. "When Annabel popped up with this dialogue, and civil society and wanting to talk about issues and come together in the middle, particularly when she wanted to talk to somebody like me, just an independent voter—that impressed me, so I thought I'd follow the movement."

Al Alborn is the kind of guy who likes a bottom line. And right about now, this is his:

"It's about understanding where America wants to go."

💀 JIM JONES, THE NUT

Since he began a cult of his very own with the Peoples Temple—which may well leave a larger footprint in history than either the Tea or Coffee parties ever will—JIM JONES deserves a mention here among the beverage crowd.

Jones's life and ideals—for good or ill—would have caused a gnashing of teeth in both groups. He and his wife, Marceline, had what he called a "rainbow family" of adopted children of several nationalities, he was a firm believer in Communism, and he certainly saw himself as a savior of his people. As with many politicians, naysayers and ex-fans would later say he led his people down the garden path—in his case, to their deaths (seems there's a health care reform lesson in here somewhere).

> 66 We have to legislate to the dumbest and craziest among us. 99
>
> —JON STEWART, THE DAILY SHOW

He also had Rep. Leo Ryan killed, the only congressman ever to be murdered in the line of duty. And aside from natural disasters and September 11, 2001, Jim Jones caused the greatest loss of life among American civilians in a single event in history.

A final lesson: This is a man who sold pet monkeys door-to-door for a living to raise money for his cause. Anything can happen.

CAPTAIN AMERICA, THE SUPERHERO

That's right—the Tea Party shenanigans have gotten so colorful that the comics have gone after them, in the guise of . . . CAPTAIN AMERICA!

In issue #602, entitled "Two Americas," Captain America and his sidekick, the Falcon, are seen in mufti checking out a political rally. The Falcon—who happens to be an African American superhero—observes that he likely would not fit in with the crowd, "a bunch of angry white folks." Seen in the mob? Protest signs reading, "Stop the socialists," "No to new taxes," and—wait for it!—"Tea bag libs before they tea bag you."

A graphic outcry ensued. One miffed conservative blogger accused Marvel of "making patriotic Americans into your newest super villains." And then Marvel—a Disney company, by the way—did what Captain America would never have done. They backed down, saying there had been a "lettering error" as the book went to press.

Seriously, Marvel? Who knew that the first place the First Amendment would fall would be the comic books?

SIGNS
&
SLOGANS

SIGNS FROM THE **TEA PARTY**

Is it their anger that makes the Teabaggers misspell? Or their rush to judgment that makes them careless? Either way, the signs and pickets they've been toting around from coast to coast have introduced a whole new word to our political vocabulary:

TEABONICS!

SOME ARE JUST PLANE BAD SPELLING . . .

AMERICA
HELP US
BOYCOTT
MEXICO
- - - - - -
RESPECT
ARE-COUNTRY
SPEAK
ENGLISH

CONGRESS=SLAVE OWNER
TAXPAYER = NIGGAR

FEEDOM
DOESN'T COME
FREE

REPEEL CONGRESS

I'M A **MAVRIK**
HOW ABOUT YOU?

GOD
GOLD **&** GUNS
THE **INGRIEDTS** OF FREEDOM

OBAMA
LIER I-N CHIEF

GET A BRAIN! MORANS

THANK YOU **FOX NEWS**
FOR KEEPING US **INFROMED**

I AM
JOE THE PLUMMER

IF YOUR NOT
OURAGED
YOUR NOT
PAYING ATTENTION

LETS **KEEP THE TEA**
DUMP THE POLITITIONS!

**MAKE ENGLISH
AMERICA'S**
OFFICAL LANGUAGE

NO AMNETY

NO TAXES
OBAMA LOVES TAXES
BANKRUPT USA
LOVES BABY KILLING

TAXATION
THE NEW TERRORISM

PARTY LIKE
IT'S **1773**

HONK IF I'M PAYING YOUR MORTGAGE

COMRADE OBAMA
SAYS OBEY

SPEAK FOR YOURSELF OBAMA
WE ARE A CHRISTIAN NATION

NOW LOOK!! NICE PEOPLE
FORCED TO PROTEST!!
THIS MUST BE **SERIOUS**
WE CAME UNARMED...THIS TIME

**THE ONLY FAIR
TAX IS NO TAX**

**CLINGING TO
MY GOD, MY GUNS
AND MY MONEY**

RISE UP
RELOAD
REVOLT

YOUR POLITICAL GLOSSARY
STRAIGHT PRIDE

Don't get excited, LGBT and queer-friendly reader: Help is not on the way. Straight pride is not morality-adjacent to gay pride. In fact, it's just the opposite. At least one Tea Party rally took heat from the gay community and human rights groups for allowing the sale of straight pride clothing and paraphernalia.

UrbanDictionary.com, a user content–generated site selected by *Time* magazine as one of the Top 50 websites in 2008, offers this definition of straight pride:

"The perfect and normal answer to 'gay pride.' The homosexual agenda forces a 'gay pride day' every year in June. By contrast, Straight Pride happens every day, 365/24/7... People that wear Straight Pride T-shirts or organize Straight Pride rallies are attacked by homosexual activists and sometimes even censored under the false charge of intolerance. How can it be intolerant to celebrate normalcy? *Every day of the year is Straight Pride Day. Every day of the year is fag shame day.*"

And then there's the Straight Pride Facebook page, which urges fans, "Spread this page to your straight friends! And let's show that you can be straight and still be cool too!"

Yeah. Cool, Teabaggers.

HATRIOT

Though it still looks like "hat riot" to us (and that's not far from the truth), author and political pundit John Avlon has coined the word to rhyme with "patriot." Coffee Party founder Annabel Park has noted that certain media treat only the conservative right as patriots—but some believe a subset of these Americans' allegiance to the flag is born in hate and extremist behavior.

Again, turning to UrbanDictionary.com for a definition of the hatriot:

"Someone who claims to love America but hates the majority of the people who actually live there. Hatriots often romanticize small towns and rural areas, which they view as the 'Real America,' and they mistrust large cities, which are full of liberal elites, colored people, and the undeserving poor."

An interesting aside: Avlon is married to Republican President Herbert Hoover's great granddaughter, Margaret. Hoover, by the way, who served in the White House in the years before the Great Depression, had absolutely no interest in civil rights.

GOD HATES TAXES

IMPEACH THE MUSLIM MARXIST

BUY OBAMACARE!

READ MY LIPSTICK! NO MORE BAILOUTS!

COMMUNISTS ARE DEMOCRATS IN A HURRY

THE AMERICAN TAXPAYERS **ARE THE JEWS FOR OBAMA'S OVENS**

HITLER GAVE GOOD SPEECHES, TOO

I'M TEABAGGING **4 JESUS**

THROW BARNEY FRANK **UNDER THE BUS**

YOU KNOW WHY DEMOCRATS **LOVE TAXES? THEY DON'T PAY ANY!**

OBAMMUNISM **SLAVERY YOU CAN BELIEVE IN**

HEAR MY VOICE **OR** HEAR MY GUN

NAZI PELOSI YOU CAN KEEP YOUR FASCISM I'LL KEEP MY FREEDOM

SIGNS FROM THE **INTERLOPERS**

But where would politics be without spying and infiltration? Some of the most inventive and provocative messages appear on the picket signs of the impostor Teabaggers—infiltrators at Tea Party rallies trying to subvert the already tainted Tea Party reputation from the inside . . .

I'M A **BIGOT**
I'M A RACIST
I'M A **TEABAGGER**

2012 ELECT
SARAH PALIN/
PARIS HILTON
BIMBO PARTY

GENERIC
ANGRY SLOGAN

I FORGOT WHAT I'M ANGRY ABOUT

I'M GAY FOR PALIN!

GOD HATES **FOX NEWS**

TINA FEY
DOES IT BETTER

AM I FULL OF HATE, LIES & B.S.?
YOU BETCHA!

RABBLE RABBLE RABBLE RABBLE
TAXES RABBLE RABBLE RABBLE
HEALTHCARE RABBLE RABBLE
RABBLE RABBLE RABBLE RABBLE
RABBLE **COMMUNISM** RABBLE

GLENN BECK
RAPED AND **MURDERED**
A GIRL IN 1990

SIGNS FROM THE COFFEE PARTY

"Earnest" is the word that best describes the Coffee Party gang. That and "nascent." So while the Tea Partyers are road tripping in fancy tour busses, these grassroots folks are just beginning to grow, meeting in coffee shops around the country, planning, plotting, and gathering steam. They are making placards in their kaffeeklatsches, sharing their thoughts with each other, making appointments with their legislators, getting students activated on campus. Nice-nice, for now. They are not as vocal or as celebrated (yet) and bring to mind what anthropologist Margaret Mead once said—on a picket sign it would have nearly universal appeal: "A small group of thoughtful people could change the world. Indeed, it's the only thing that ever has."

SOME POLITE SIGNS FROM THE COFFEE PARTY:

THIS
"HOPEY"
"CHANGEY"
THING
IS
WORKING OUT
FOR ME

COMPASSION IS A
FAMILY VALUE

PEACE
LOVE
COFFEE

POLLING FOR DUMMIES

A CBS/*New York Times* poll published in the spring of 2010 enlightened the American public about the Tea Party's opinions—and there was some very surprising data. Much has been written about this survey, which polled 1,580 American adults. For those who missed it or found all those numbers dreary, here's an idiot's (no offense) cheat sheet to some of the more fascinating numbers:

SMARTER AND RICHER

Tea Party folks have it better than most, which makes one wonder—why the big fuss? Non–Tea Party-ers may do well to consider this: If being pissed off is the price you pay to get a better education and make more money, who wouldn't be happy to be mad? Twenty-five percent of Americans graduate from college; Tea Party followers are at 37 percent. And they've got more money! Fifty-six percent make upward of $50,000; 30 percent rake in more than $100,000.

WHY THEY'RE LIKE YOU

The majority of Tea Party people send their kids to public schools and think Sarah Palin is not qualified to be president. That's comforting . . . isn't it?

THE ROAD TO MOSCOW

More than half of Americans feel the current president is leading us down the pinko garden path; but a whopping 92 percent of the Teabaggers think we're headed toward a future in socialism.

SNORE

The typical Teabagger is white, male, Republican, married, and older than forty-five. Ooh, Daddy!

TEANUNDRUM

Though high taxes are a huge buga-boo of the Tea Partyers—in fact, April 15 is their national holiday, with Tax Day rallies their favorite form of entertainment—over half of them agree that the income tax they were levied in 2010 was fair. Could somebody remind these people what they're mad about again?

YOUR NEW CAREER

Sixty percent of Tea Partyers say, "America's best years are behind us," as far as job availability is concerned. So much for that corner office.

RACIAL PROFILER-IN-CHIEF

A quarter of the Teabaggers inter-viewed are certain that President Obama favors black people over white.

HELL IN A HANDBASKET

Nine out of ten Tea Party supporters think the country is headed in the wrong direction. Also unsettling: Six-ty percent of *all* Americans believe we're headed the wrong way, too.

SQUEAKY WHEEL LAW RULES!

Only 18 percent of those polled identify themselves as Tea Party members. What?! Then why are they on the news night and day? Irish Americans make up over 11 percent of the U.S. population, and now that Ted Kennedy's gone, you hardly ever hear a thing about *them*.

READY, AIM . . .

Just be careful with your opinions, Anyone with Other Ideas. Fifty-eight percent of Teabaggers own a gun.

PARTY POLITICS, DISSECTED

Sometimes a picture (or two) is truly
worth a thousand words . . .

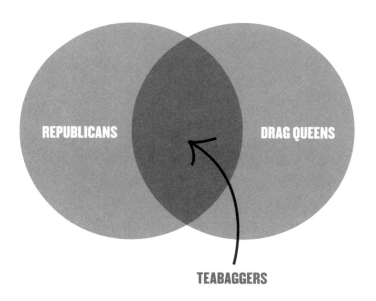

REPUBLICANS

DRAG QUEENS

TEABAGGERS

DOES THIS TRICORNERED HAT MATCH MY GUN?

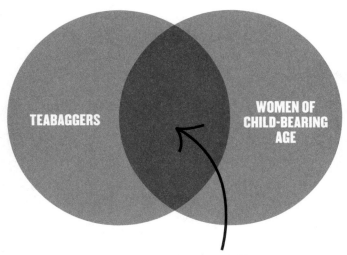

TEABAGGERS

WOMEN OF
CHILD-BEARING
AGE

DAUGHTERS OF PARENTS FROM THE
RELIGIOUS RIGHT WHO WILL NEED
FEDERALLY FUNDED ABORTIONS

MORALITY: DOES IT CHANGE WHEN IT'S YOU?

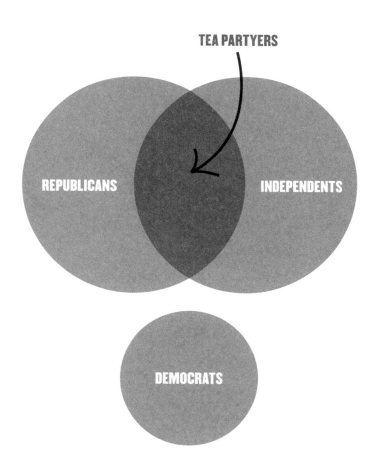

CURRENT STATE OF AMERICAN POLITICS

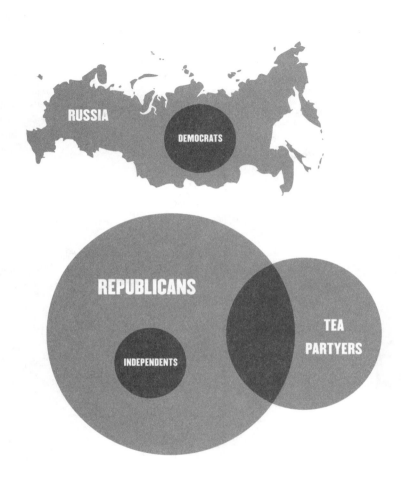

RUSSIA

DEMOCRATS

REPUBLICANS

TEA PARTYERS

INDEPENDENTS

REPUBLICANS' DREAM

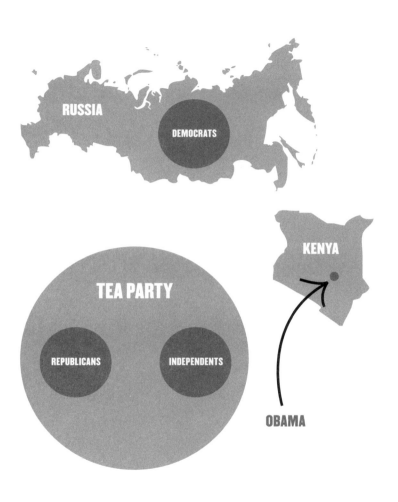

RUSSIA

DEMOCRATS

KENYA

TEA PARTY

REPUBLICANS

INDEPENDENTS

OBAMA

TEABAGGERS' DREAM

CHOOSE
YOUR
POISON

Which brew's for you? Sometimes, in a tough election season, it really helps to just sit down and make a checklist of the things that appeal to you about each party. Perhaps this will help.

TEA PARTY CHECKLIST

- [ ] I am against the health care reform bill, but 100% for my own Social Security and Medicare coverage.

- [ ] I believe American jobs are for Americans, whether they want them or not.

- [ ] I believe taxes are higher under this Democratic president, no matter what the *New York Times* says.

- [ ] I am all for stem cell research, as long as the genetic material is preselected according to political affiliation.

- [ ] I believe pro-life means more paid vacation.

- [ ] I believe that Wall Street will figure things out; after all, some of those bankers are my best friends!

- [ ] I believe astroturfing is a figment of the liberal imagination.

- [ ] I think that there's nothing like a good spit and an epithet to cleanse the soul.

- [ ] I believe papers should be checked for all foreign-looking individuals, including a certain resident of 1600 Pennsylvania Avenue NW in Washington, D.C.

- [ ] I believe marching in colonial costume is sexy and debonair.

COFFEE PARTY CHECKLIST

- [ ] I say no to filibusters; for that matter, no yelling, either.

- [ ] I think Wall Street should be made into a nice pedestrian mall.

- [ ] I think someone should offer Sarah Palin a one-way ticket to a desert island. Glenn Beck should get that travel package, too.

- [ ] I say change we can believe in takes place through civil discourse, following the lead of people like Martin Luther King Jr. and Gandhi. Or even in complete silence, like Clarabell the Clown.

- [ ] I believe lobbying from the heart can be as successful as lobbying from the wallet.

- [ ] If Emily Post were running for Congress, I would vote for her.

- [ ] I think there's no reason to gallivant around the country on a fancy tour bus when we have a nice vegan cafe to meet in right here in the neighborhood.

- [ ] I believe that in America we care for each other, no matter what it does to my taxes.

- [ ] I know that earnest planning in small groups is the most effective road to change.

- [ ] "Wake Up and Stand Up" is my mantra: I truly believe that Peace, Love, and Coffee can conquer the world.

YOUR POLITICAL SCORECARD

As we close in on Election Day, the issues inevitably become more and more confusing. Lies are told, political favors traded, party lines crossed. Sometimes it just seems like you can't remember what the important issues are and where your candidate even stands anymore. And so, a short scorecard, with space to fill in the names of your local favorites on the issues you love to hate:

WALL STREET REFORM

TAXES—FAIR OR UNFAIR?

GOVERNMENT ACCOUNTABILITY

BEST CRANK CALLS

GUN-TOTING AND WOLF-HUNTING

OFFERS BEST FREE TCHOTCHKES

FURTHEST FROM/CLOSEST TO
NEW SOCIALISM MACHINE

SEEMS LEAST AFFECTED BY LOBBYING

IMMIGRATION REFORM

BEST ALL-AROUND CHOICES FOR
KEEPING ME SAFE AND SOUND

DRESSES LIKE I DRESS

OTHER ISSUES:

CAMPAIGN REFORM

ACKNOWLEDGMENTS

For my parents, who, like many couples, spent their entire married lives canceling out each other's votes.

To Senator Jack Fitzpatrick of Massachusetts, who dropped me on a doorstep in Pittsfield and taught me to start knocking.

To the Empire State Pride Agenda, who taught me Gay Is Good and made me get out there and fight for it.

For every politician who made me angry.

For every change for the better that made me cry.

And to my friends at Abrams, especially Mary Wowk for the big idea and David Cashion for making it real.

ABOUT THE AUTHOR

Erin McHugh is a former publishing executive and the author of nearly twenty books. She first went canvassing door to door for a political candidate when she was still too young to vote. Erin splits her time between New York City and South Dartmouth, MA.